Oboe Carol T

12 best-loved carols for the young oboist

Arranged for easy oboe and piano
by Robert Hinchliffe

Faber Music
London

Arrangements © 1991 by Faber Music Ltd
First published in 1991 by Faber Music Ltd
3 Queen Square London WC1N 3AU
Music drawn by Sambo Music Engraving Co
Cover illustration by Penny Dann
Cover design by Shirley Tucker
Printed in England

ISBN 0 571 51228 3

CONTENTS

1.   While shepherds watched their flocks by night

2. Away in a manger

3.   Good King Wenceslas

4. O come, all ye faithful

5.   Angels from the realms of glory

4.   O come, all ye faithful

5.   Angels from the realms of glory

6.   O little town of Bethlehem

Oboe Carol Time

Arranged by Robert Hinchliffe

1.   While shepherds watched their flocks by night

2.   Away in a manger

3.   Good King Wenceslas

4

10.   Silent night

11.   Jingle bells

* In the piano part this final section is printed in full (bars 21-36).

12.   Joy to the world

Reproduced and printed by Halstan & Co. Ltd., Amersham, Bucks., England

7. The first Nowell

8. See amid the winter's snow

9. Once in royal David's city

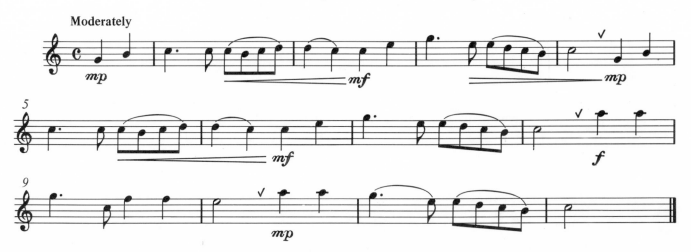

6. O little town of Bethlehem

7. The first Nowell

8.   See amid the winter's snow

10

9.   Once in royal David's city

10.   Silent night

11. Jingle bells

13

* grace notes optional

14

12. Joy to the world

Reproduced and printed by Halstan & Co. Ltd., Amersham, Bucks., England